$\mathcal{D}$EVOTIONS

for

SUNDAY

SCHOOL

TEACHERS

DEVOTIONS
for
SUNDAY
SCHOOL
TEACHERS

Stan Toler
&
John Baldwin

Beacon Hill Press of Kansas City
Kansas City, Missouri

Copyright 2002
by Beacon Hill Press of Kansas City

ISBN 083-412-0011

Printed in the
United States of America

Cover Design: Marie Tabler

Library of Congress Cataloging-in-Publication Data

Toler, Stan.
 Devotions for Sunday school teachers / Stan Toler, John Baldwin.
   p. cm.
 ISBN 0-8341-2001-1
 1. Sunday school teachers—Prayer-books and devotions—English. I. Baldwin, John, 1950-   . II. Title.
 BV4596.S9T65 2002
 242'.69—dc21

2002008954

10 9 8 7 6 5 4 3 2

To the Sunday School teachers at Trinity Church of the Nazarene in Oklahoma City. Thank you for your faithfulness each week in teaching to influence lives. You're the greatest, and you are loved!
—Stan Toler

To Glenda, my best friend of 36 years and my dear wife of 33 years. I have eagerly looked forward to dedicating my first book to you. Thank you for loving me, believing in me, and showing me the way to live.
—John Baldwin

Contents

Foreword 9

Acknowledgments 11

Discouragement 13

Eternal Impact 15

Lesson Closing 17

Sunday School Teachers and Pastors 19

Perseverance 21

Primary Objective 23

Priorities 25

Sweaty Palms 27

Tools of My Trade 29

Visitors 31

Passion 33

Quiet Time 35

Follow-up 37

Prayer 39

Trolling or Fishing? 41

Preparation 43

Distractions 45

Encouragement 47

Shepherding 49

Whose Sheep Are These? 51

Disappointment 53

Eloquence 55

Timing 57

In the Fiery Furnace 59

Sower or Harvester?   61
Topics   63
A Singular Question   65
Theology   67
Helping My Pastor   69
Salvation   71
Example   73
Sanctification   75
Study   77
The Race   79
Making a Difference   81
The Crown   83
The Master Teacher   85
Victory   87
Small Groups   89
Focus   91
Holiness   93
Methods or Ministry?   95
Surroundings   97
Show and Tell   99
Generation to Generation   101
Cross Culture   103
Tears   105
Relief Efforts   107
Loving Influence   109
Breaking Through the Wall   111
About the Authors   112

FOREWORD

Stan Toler and John Baldwin have partnered in providing an excellent source of inspiration for Sunday School teachers. Toler, a practitioner as a pastor and presenter of "principles of excellence" for teachers, joins with Baldwin, a layman with a passion for God, the church, and especially Sunday School, in producing this great work.

It was Henrietta Mears who said, "Don't ever say, 'I'm just a Sunday School teacher.' You may be the link between an individual's life and his or her eternal destiny."

Toler and Baldwin have teamed up to bring to the truly dedicated teacher words of hope and special encouragement. Sunday School teachers desiring to make a real connection with people for Christ will use this book often as a source of renewal and spiritual uplift. It will further enhance a teacher in preparation for effective teaching.

—W. Talmadge Johnson

ACKNOWLEDGMENTS

Special thanks to Jerry Brecheisen, Lawrence Wilson, Pat Diamond, Deloris Leonard, Bonnie Perry, Hardy Weathers, Bruce Nuffer, Paul Martin, and the whole Beacon Hill team.

—Stan Toler

Many thanks to Peggy Lewis and Jeff Brock for your valuable contributions, insightful suggestions, and personal efforts to make this project a success. Both of you constantly inspire me to a closer and deeper walk with our Savior. Thank you to the Sunday School teachers and staff of Highland Park Church of the Nazarene in Lakeland, Florida. Your reward in heaven will be great indeed.

—John Baldwin

I ASK YOU, THEREFORE, NOT TO
BE DISCOURAGED BECAUSE OF
MY SUFFERINGS FOR YOU,
WHICH ARE YOUR GLORY.
—Eph. 3:13

WHEN WE YIELD TO DISCOURAGEMENT,
IT IS USUALLY BECAUSE WE GIVE TOO
MUCH THOUGHT TO THE PAST
OR TO THE FUTURE.
—Therese of Lisieux

DISCOURAGEMENT

*C*fter testing more than 1,600 materials and filling over 40,000 pages of laboratory notes, Thomas Edison finally identified a material (carbonized bamboo) that would burn for at least 40 hours as an electric light bulb filament. It took him another three years to perfect a bulb for residential use. That was in 1882. Today you can see Edison's handmade bulbs still burning at his winter house in Fort Myers, Florida. For at least 1,600 consecutive times, Edison was disappointed. Was it discouraging? Undoubtedly. But his discouragement led to discovery, not defeat.

Paul knew how the wear and tear of ministry could discourage believers. So he reminded us that discouragement could be turned to discovery—the discovery of God's glorious presence and His eternal purpose. Paul learned how to content himself in the Lord no matter the external circumstances.

Let Christ turn your discouragements into His eternal hope.

Prayer: *Lord, help me to discover Your loving presence and Your eternal purpose, even in the discouraging times. In Christ's name. Amen.*

Based on Paul's letter to Timothy

I HAVE BEEN REMINDED OF YOUR SINCERE
FAITH, WHICH FIRST LIVED IN YOUR
GRANDMOTHER LOIS AND IN YOUR
MOTHER EUNICE AND, I AM PERSUADED,
NOW LIVES IN YOU ALSO.
—2 Tim. 1:5

WHEN I THINK OF THOSE WHO HAVE
INFLUENCED MY LIFE THE MOST, I THINK
NOT OF THE GREAT BUT OF THE GOOD.
—John Knox

Eternal Impact

Only eternity will reveal the final impact of your ministry. Consider Sunday School teacher Edward Kimball. One April Saturday in 1855, he walked into Holton's Shoe Store in Boston looking for one of the boys in his senior high class. Finding him in the stockroom wrapping shoes, Kimball put his arm around the 18-year-old and said, "Let me tell you how much Christ loves you." They knelt together, and the teenager was saved. His name? Dwight L. Moody.

Years later, J. Wilbur Chapman was called to ministry under Moody's preaching. Chapman became an evangelist and hired former baseball player Billy Sunday. In 1924 evangelist Billy Sunday held a revival in Charlotte, North Carolina. A men's prayer group grew out of it. In 1934 they invited evangelist Mordecai Ham to hold a revival, where two teenaged boys responded to an invitation: Grady Wilson and Billy Graham.

Kimball's faithfulness to his call as a Sunday School teacher resulted in the salvation of a young man 79 years later whose ministry has reached millions. Someday you will know how your ministry impacted others for Jesus.

Prayer: *Lord, thank You for the enduring influence of my teaching ministry. In Jesus' name. Amen.*

"SIRS, WHAT MUST I DO TO BE SAVED?"
THEY REPLIED, "BELIEVE IN THE LORD
JESUS, AND YOU WILL BE SAVED—
YOU AND YOUR HOUSEHOLD."
—Acts 16:30-31

THE TEACHER SENT FROM GOD IS THE
ONE WHO CLEARS THE WAY TO JESUS
AND KEEPS IT CLEAR.
—Oswald Chambers

LESSON CLOSING

On Sunday evening, October 8, 1871, D. L. Moody was preaching a message on Pilate. As he came to the end of his sermon, he turned to Matt. 27:22 and read Pilate's famous question: "What shall I do, then, with Jesus who is called Christ?" Moody said to the packed sanctuary, "Take this text home with you and turn it over in your minds during this week. Next Sabbath we will come to Calvary and the Cross, and we will decide what to do with Jesus of Nazareth."

As beloved songwriter and singer Ira Sankey sang the final hymn, fire engines could be heard in the streets. The great Chicago fire had begun. Soon 300 souls would perish. Moody never saw that congregation again. He called the conclusion to that service the worst mistake he ever made as a preacher. Never again did he speak without calling his hearers to make a decision about Christ.

We must never forfeit an opportunity to press the claims of the gospel. Every time you speak of the gospel, offer this greatest of God's gifts to your hearers.

Prayer: *Lord, remind me to always give my students an opportunity to come to know You as Savior and Sanctifier. In Your name I pray. Amen.*

OBEY YOUR LEADERS AND SUBMIT TO
THEIR AUTHORITY. THEY KEEP WATCH
OVER YOU AS MEN WHO MUST GIVE AN
ACCOUNT. OBEY THEM SO THAT THEIR
WORK WILL BE A JOY, NOT A BURDEN,
FOR THAT WOULD BE OF NO ADVANTAGE
TO YOU.
—Heb. 13:17

ONE OF THE MARKS OF TRUE GREATNESS
IS THE ABILITY TO DEVELOP
GREATNESS IN OTHERS.
—J. C. MaCaulay

Sunday School
Teachers and Pastors

 atthew tells us our Lord was astonished the day He encountered a Roman centurion with faith and understanding of order and authority (Matt. 8:10). This army officer knew Jesus didn't have to go to his home to heal his servant—the Lord's word and authority alone would bring about the miracle.

This centurion obeyed Christ's orders, just as he obeyed orders from Rome.

Paul told the Corinthian church that orderliness and authority are important in the Kingdom too (1 Cor. 14:40). Our pastors are our spiritual and organizational leaders. The message we Sunday School teachers give our classes each week must always be doctrinally and practically consistent with the pastor's words from the pulpit. We're under our pastor's authority through Christ.

While Sunday School teachers and pastors alike are called to share the gospel, your pastor is uniquely ordained by God to lead the local church. Be your pastor's biggest supporter!

Prayer: *Lord, thank You for the teamwork between the pulpit and the classroom. Bless our work together for the advancement of Your kingdom. In Christ's name I pray. Amen.*

THEREFORE, MY DEAR BROTHERS,
STAND FIRM. LET NOTHING MOVE YOU.
ALWAYS GIVE YOURSELVES FULLY TO THE
WORK OF THE LORD, BECAUSE YOU
KNOW THAT YOUR LABOR IN THE LORD
IS NOT IN VAIN.
—1 Cor. 15:58

PRESS ON! NOTHING IN THE WORLD
CAN TAKE THE PLACE OF PERSEVERANCE.
—Calvin Coolidge

PERSEVERANCE

Well over an hour after the 1968 Olympic marathon winners had been crowned, the few thousand spectators remaining in Mexico City's stadium witnessed an astonishing event. Into the arena hobbled a lone figure wearing the colors of Tanzania. One of his legs was bloodied and bandaged from a severe knee injury sustained earlier in the 26.2-mile race. He grimaced with every labored step but resolutely made his way around the 400-meter track toward the finish line. The crowd began to cheer, softly at first, then thunderously as he crossed the finish line—dead last and in excruciating pain. His name was John Akhwari.

Reporters rushed to him in amazement. They wanted to know why he had not quit miles ago. He answered, "My country did not send me 7,000 miles away to start the race. They sent me 7,000 miles to finish it."

Jesus similarly calls us to persevere. He tells us to go, to make disciples, to baptize, and to teach. Lest we become weary, He reminds us that He will be with us to the ends of the earth and time. With His call always comes His enabling. He will never leave us or forsake us.

Prayer: *Lord, when I'm tempted to quit, help me remember that You persevered for my salvation. And help me remember that I'll never run the race alone. In Your name I pray. Amen.*

DO YOUR BEST TO PRESENT YOURSELF TO
GOD AS ONE APPROVED, A WORKMAN
WHO DOES NOT NEED TO BE ASHAMED
AND WHO CORRECTLY HANDLES THE
WORD OF TRUTH.
—2 Tim. 2:15

A MAN'S HEART HAS ONLY ENOUGH LIFE
IN IT TO PURSUE ONE OBJECT FULLY.
—Charles Haddon Spurgeon

PRIMARY OBJECTIVE

*D*uring the year 2000, business bankruptcies in the United States were filed on an average of one every 3.5 minutes. Mismanagement by company owners is cited as the most frequent cause of business bankruptcies. Economists cite lack of direction as the best example of mismanagement. What in the world is lack of direction?

It's what occurs when a company's owners have no clear business plan in mind with measurable, well-reasoned goals, objectives, and priorities. Most owners and managers of bankrupt businesses could not verbalize their No. 1 reason for being in business. When the storms of economic challenges came along, they didn't know what to do because they didn't know where they were going.

What's your primary objective as a Sunday School teacher? What's the No. 1 reason your Sunday School class exists? Paul's advice to young Timothy reminds us—we must correctly handle the word of truth. Know it, meditate on it, cherish it, and teach it with skill and compassion.

Paul's advice to Timothy in our Scripture reading today sums it up best!

Prayer: *Lord, thank You for Your eternal Word. Help me both faithfully learn it and faithfully teach it. In Jesus' name I pray. Amen.*

THE VERY WORK THAT THE FATHER
HAS GIVEN ME TO FINISH, AND WHICH
I AM DOING, TESTIFIES THAT THE
FATHER HAS SENT ME.
—John 5:36

BE ABOUT YOUR FATHER'S BUSINESS.
THERE WILL ALWAYS BE PLENTY OF
OTHER PEOPLE OCCUPIED WITH
THE AFFAIRS OF THE WORLD.
—Frances J. Roberts

PRIORITIES

Al invited his friend to go flying. It was his friend's first experience in a single-engine, four-seat airplane. They spent almost 20 minutes making sure there was no water in the plane's fuel, checking the oil level, inspecting each flap and wing, examining the tires, and going over safety procedures.

Then when Al started the engine, he and his new "copilot" went through another, even longer, checklist—twice! Finally they pulled out onto the runway, lowered the flaps, and under full throttle, soared into a beautiful Florida afternoon sky. A couple of hours later, as the sun set over the bay, they landed safely.

As an experienced pilot, Al knew the priorities that must be rigidly observed to fly safely. A pilot can overlook precious few details in planning a flight. The same is true for Sunday School teachers.

Jesus was always very clear about His priorities. He overlooked no detail of His call and called His disciples (and us) to the same holy standard. Are your priorities in order?

Prayer: *Lord, may Your Holy Spirit constantly go over my checklist with me—deleting and adding, until nothing is left but Your perfect will for my life and ministry. In Your holy name I pray. Amen.*

Moses said to the LORD, "O Lord,
I have never been eloquent,
neither in the past nor since you
have spoken to your servant. I am
slow of speech and tongue."
—Exod. 4:10

The remarkable thing about
fearing God is that when you fear
God, you fear nothing else,
whereas if you do not fear God,
you fear everything else.
—Oswald Chambers

SWEATY PALMS

August 1983 is burned into one Sunday School teacher's memory. He was a new instructor standing before a college finance class with the eyes of all 63 students fixed upon him. His throat was dry. His eyes burned. His breath was short and shallow. His palms were sweaty. Almost 20 years later, He could tell you what He was wearing that momentous day. Why did this experience affect him so?

He was exhibiting the classic symptoms of speaker's fright. This emotion befalls the person who is fearful of speaking in public. Some people rank it right alongside death as their worst fear.

Moses had speaker's fright when the Lord called him. But God was with him, putting the proper words in his mouth when it came time for him to speak. Many of us Sunday School teachers suffer from varying degrees of the same phobia. But God promises to be with us. We prepare our lessons diligently, hone our teaching skills, and speak before our classes with humble reliance on His strength and provision.

Prayer: *Lord, thank You for Your faithfulness in giving me the right words at the right time. I pray in Jesus' name. Amen.*

THE WORD OF GOD IS LIVING AND
ACTIVE. SHARPER THAN ANY DOUBLE-
EDGED SWORD, IT PENETRATES EVEN TO
DIVIDING SOUL AND SPIRIT, JOINTS AND
MARROW; IT JUDGES THE THOUGHTS
AND ATTITUDES OF THE HEART.
—Heb. 4:12

IT IS NOT POSSIBLE EVER TO EXHAUST
THE MIND OF THE SCRIPTURES. IT IS A
WELL THAT HAS NO BOTTOM.
—John Chrysostom

TOOLS OF MY TRADE

The young man was an Air Force camera repair technician during the Korean War. This trade served him well after the war as well. With it he worked his way through college and seminary, becoming a pastor and later a college professor. He often plied his camera repair trade to support his family. His toolbox was large, heavy, square, and black. Its thin felt-lined drawers were full of small, shiny precision tools of all shapes and designs. Each had a specific application. Together they were needed to do a good job repairing cameras.

As Sunday School teachers, we, too, have a toolbox: God's Holy Word. God himself furnished it. Everything we will ever need for any job is within it—every truth, every promise, every warning, every encouragement, and every direction.

The Bible is your complete toolbox. Always keep it handy. Let the Holy Spirit teach you how to use His tools. Exercise them often and well. Never neglect them or toss them aside carelessly. Keep them in good repair.

On that final day, you and I will be judged on how well we used the tools at our disposal to advance the kingdom of God.

Prayer: *Lord, with the kind of skill You possessed as a carpenter, help me to use the toolbox of Your eternal Word to build and repair lives. In Your holy name I pray. Amen.*

Seated in a window was a young
man named Eutychus, who was
sinking into a deep sleep as
Paul talked on and on.
—Acts 20:9

When there is room in the heart
there is room in the house.
—Danish Proverb

VISITORS

Great American wit Groucho Marx once sent this short letter to a social organization: "Please accept my resignation. I don't care to belong to a club that accepts people like me as members."

Have you ever carefully thought about the impression your Sunday School class makes on visitors? If you were new to your church, would you want to attend your Sunday School class again after visiting it once?

One of Paul's lengthy sermons and the lateness of the hour combined to put one of his visitors soundly asleep. Unfortunately, the visiting lad was perched in a third-story window and upon falling asleep fell to his death. God's touch through Paul's prayer quickly brought him back to life, but there's a valuable lesson here for Sunday School teachers: if we put a visitor to sleep in our class, would we even know it?

Do we enthusiastically welcome visitors and make them feel comfortable? Do we follow up and invite them back? Do we extend the same measure of hospitality to them we would expect? Remember: there was a day when each of us was a visitor in Christ's presence.

Aren't you glad He welcomed us warmly?

Prayer: *Lord, may my hospitality and my heartfelt enthusiasm make You even more attractive to the visitors in my class. In Jesus' name I pray. Amen.*

JESUS REPLIED, "LET US GO SOMEWHERE
ELSE—TO THE NEARBY VILLAGES—
SO I CAN PREACH THERE ALSO.
THAT IS WHY I HAVE COME."
—Mark 1:38

A MAN CAN SUCCEED AT ALMOST
ANYTHING FOR WHICH HE HAS
UNLIMITED ENTHUSIASM.
—Charles M. Schwab

PASSION

What do you love to do? Everyone has a passion, from golf to gross national product to garage sales. Each of us has something that dominates our thoughts and actions. Having trouble identifying yours? If so, take a look at your planning book and your credit card receipts. Where you spend your time and resources almost always indicates where your interests are.

Jesus didn't have a planning book or a credit card. But He had a passion. Jesus' passion was to preach the Good News—anytime and anywhere He could. As a child, He wandered away from His parents and was found ministering in the Temple. "'Why were you searching for me?' he asked. 'Didn't you know I had to be in my Father's house?'" (Luke 2:49). During His adult ministry, His every move had a preaching purpose: "Now he had to go through Samaria" (John 4:4). There He taught the woman at the well about a spiritual supply that would meet all the needs of her thirsting heart.

Do you have a passion to preach the Good News everywhere you go—on the job, in the home, in your church? Are you anxious for the next opportunity to share God's truth with your class? Do you get excited when Sunday's coming?

Pray for a *passion* to teach the Word of God.

Prayer: *Lord, thank You for revealing Your passion to preach the Good News. I pray that You will fill my heart and my mind with a holy zeal to share Your holiness and Your forgiveness with my class. In Your name I pray. Amen.*

VERY EARLY IN THE MORNING,
WHILE IT WAS STILL DARK, JESUS GOT UP,
LEFT THE HOUSE AND WENT OFF TO A
SOLITARY PLACE, WHERE HE PRAYED.
—Mark 1:35

YIELD ROOM FOR SOME LITTLE TIME TO
GOD, AND REST FOR A LITTLE TIME IN
HIM. ENTER THE INNER CHAMBER OF
THY MIND; SHUT OUT ALL THOUGHTS
SAVE THAT OF GOD AND SUCH AS
CAN AID THEE IN SEEKING HIM.
—Saint Anselm

QUIET TIME

What does your Sunday morning look like—a blaring alarm, a quick cup of coffee, a glance at the lesson, and then a mad dash to church? That Sunday morning dash may lead to a crash, in more ways than one! But certainly it's a disaster in the making for your Sunday School class. You (and your students) will soon tire of dealing with ministry in such an ill-planned manner.

Jesus knew the value of quiet time. He used moments alone to center himself in the Father and on His mission—nothing hurried, but systematic, focused, solitary times of reaching out to the Heavenly Father for instruction and inspiration.

You and your class deserve nothing less. The times you spend alone with the Master Teacher will enrich your own soul. Getting His Word first in your heart will enable you to share it with others. Your class will know when you've been with the Lord. It will be in your heart as well as on your face and in your attitude. And it will spill into your class presentation.

If you can't find a quiet time, then make one.

Prayer: *Lord, help me to understand that I'm not prepared to represent You until, first of all, I've spent time with You. In Your name I pray. Amen.*

THEN JESUS SAID TO HIM, "SEE THAT YOU
DON'T TELL ANYONE. BUT GO, SHOW
YOURSELF TO THE PRIEST AND OFFER
THE GIFT MOSES COMMANDED, AS A
TESTIMONY TO THEM."
—Matt. 8:4

A PERSON MAY CAUSE EVIL TO OTHERS
NOT ONLY BY HIS ACTIONS BUT
BY HIS INACTION, AND IN EITHER CASE
HE IS JUSTLY ACCOUNTABLE TO THEM
FOR THE INJURY.
—John Stuart Mill

FOLLOW-UP

*I*t was a great class. You prepared well. The students partici-
pated. The discussion was meaningful. Now your students
are headed for the worship service. Class is over, right?

Maybe not. There's often one more thing that needs to be
done.

Carla brought a friend today. She'll need a contact this
week that says, "I'm glad you came."

Matt's dad is having surgery on Thursday. He'll need
prayer, a card, and perhaps a visit.

Jerry was excited about applying today's truth to his work.
He may need a contact that says, "So how did it go on the
job?"

The lesson doesn't end when the bell rings. That's when it
starts! Truth doesn't have four walls and a whiteboard. It isn't
limited to that space of time before or after the worship service. Truth is mobile. Your students take it with them—to
their homes, to their jobs, to their schools.

So the truth-teller has a range of responsibility wider than
just the classroom. He or she is responsible for applying its
mercy, grace, or conviction in person. That conversation on
the phone may be even more effective than the question-and-
answer session in class. That card or letter or visit may have
an even greater impact than the chart on the wall or the over-
head. Think about the follow-up.

Prayer: *Lord, show me how to take Your truth to the streets where
my students live. In Jesus' name I pray. Amen.*

THE PRAYER OF A RIGHTEOUS MAN
IS POWERFUL AND EFFECTIVE.
—James 5:16

THE WHOLE THREEFOLD LIFE OF THE
THREE-PERSONAL BEING IS ACTUALLY
GOING ON IN THAT ORDINARY LITTLE
BEDROOM WHERE AN ORDINARY MAN
IS SAYING HIS PRAYERS.
—C. S. Lewis

PRAYER

*g*t's a tough world out there. That's never more apparent than during a Sunday School "prayer and share" time. Alcoholic husbands, demanding bosses, sick children, bill collectors: they all show up in Sunday School—not in person, but personified as prayer requests.

Here's the good news. Prayer works. It softens a husband's bitterness. It lightens the office atmosphere. It moves the Great Physician to His providential healing. It supplies financial needs.

Never begin a lesson without prayer—not just for yourself, but for your students as well. Their 9-to-5s are filled with pressures. Their after-hours are often covered with trials and tears. They need a "huddle" before they go out onto the playing field. They need to see that their coach/teacher believes that words and phrases sent toward heaven in faith can put heaven on "highest alert."

Pray before you get to class. Bring your students to Jesus. Nothing you tell Him will be news. But the telling expresses your confidence that your prayers move Him with compassion.

Pray with your class. Prayer is their safety valve. Prayer is a reminder of their community of faith.

Pray in closing. Let the last word of your class be a word to the Father. Discover the power of prayer—together.

Pray: *Lord, teach me to pray just as You taught Your disciples to pray. Give me the boldness to take the needs of my class before Your throne in faith, believing that the answer is imminent. In Your wonderful name I pray. Amen.*

SIMON ANSWERED, "MASTER, WE'VE
WORKED HARD ALL NIGHT AND HAVEN'T
CAUGHT ANYTHING. BUT BECAUSE YOU
SAY SO, I WILL LET DOWN THE NETS."
—Luke 5:5

IN AN EFFORT TO GET THE WORK OF
THE LORD DONE WE OFTEN LOSE
CONTACT WITH THE LORD OF THE
WORK AND QUITE LITERALLY WEAR
OUR PEOPLE OUT AS WELL.
—A. W. Tozer

TROLLING OR FISHING?

There's a difference between trolling and fishing. Trollers cast a line or two and lazily work their way along the shore in no particular hurry. If there happens to be a fish in the neighborhood, the troller may catch it.

In contrast, good fishers are on a mission. They know where the fish are, or at least where they're likely to be, and they go after them. They may get "skunked" once in a while but not often. They're purposeful about what they're doing, and they're successful most of the time.

When you teach Sunday School, are you trolling or fishing? Do you amble along, hoping for that occasional nibble? Or are you working a plan? Have you checked your bait? Is your lesson plan interesting, informed, and inspired? How's your attitude? Are you as patient as you are persistent?

How's your plan? Are you willing to fish "smarter"? Are you willing to try new equipment? Are you willing to use different "lures"? Do you concentrate more on casting than reeling in? The disciples were trollers—until they met Jesus. Then they became "fishers of men."

Prayer: *Lord, put urgency in my spirit—urgency that will cause me to do nothing less than my best to be a fisher of men. In Your name I pray. Amen.*

SUPPOSE ONE OF YOU WANTS TO BUILD A
TOWER. WILL HE NOT FIRST SIT DOWN
AND ESTIMATE THE COST TO SEE IF HE
HAS ENOUGH MONEY TO COMPLETE IT?
—Luke 14:28

DUTY DONE IS THE SOUL'S FIRESIDE.
—Robert Browning

PREPARATION

*P*reparation is a key factor for success in any endeavor—including teaching a Sunday School class. Sure, there will be occasions when the Spirit moves and produces a great class even though you weren't prepared. But week in and week out, solid teaching results from solid preparation: sitting down, estimating needs, surveying materials, and building a plan in prayer.

Are you ready? Here's what you can do to prepare: First, pray. Communion with God is one of the greatest steps in planning to communicate with others. As the Holy Spirit impresses the needs of your class on your heart, the methods for meeting those needs will begin to unfold.

Read the Word consistently. Paul advised Pastor Timothy to "preach the Word" (2 Tim. 4:2). But along with the preaching assignment, he gave him a study assignment: "Do your best to present yourself to God as one approved, a workman who does not need to be ashamed and who correctly handles the word of truth" (2 Tim. 2:15). Correct handling of God's Word begins with familiarity with God's Word.

Set aside a regular time for lesson preparation. A pattern of diligent preparation is important to well-planned teaching. Plan your lesson early in the week. Set a midweek review, and concentrate on lesson details (including life illustrations and audiovisuals). Remember: preparation helps avoid perspiration!

Prayer: *Lord, You are the greatest teacher ever! Guide me in preparing to communicate the truths of Your Word with my class. In Your name I pray. Amen.*

THE PHARISEES AND SADDUCEES CAME TO JESUS AND TESTED HIM BY ASKING HIM TO SHOW THEM A SIGN FROM HEAVEN. HE REPLIED, . . . "A WICKED AND ADULTEROUS GENERATION LOOKS FOR A MIRACULOUS SIGN, BUT NONE WILL BE GIVEN IT EXCEPT THE SIGN OF JONAH." JESUS THEN LEFT THEM AND WENT AWAY.

—Matt. 16:1-2, 4

NOTHING IS SO FATIGUING AS THE ETERNAL HANGING ON OF AN UNCOMPLETED TASK.

—William James

Distractions

*J*esus never allowed himself to be distracted from His mission. When people tried to lure Him off course, He refused to let that happen.

You'll face many distractions as a Sunday School teacher. They'll begin on Monday and continue through Sunday's class time. "Urgent" matters will pull you away from your preparation. "Once-in-a-lifetime opportunities" will beckon you on the weekend. But for the sake of your mission, there will be times when you'll simply have to say no.

You'll also face distractions *during* your class time—disruptive behavior, off-the-wall questions, "important" topics suggested for class discussion in place of the Word. You'll need to remember that you're not only a teacher—you're a guide as well. Part of your assignment is to keep your class on the right path. To do this, in your heart and by your actions you'll have to say no.

With a heart set on serving the Lord in your classroom and with a mind focused on teaching God's Word, you'll be less likely to be drawn away from the task at hand.

Remember that you've been commissioned for duty. Anything that keeps you from fulfilling your assignment is your enemy. Charge on valiantly!

Prayer: *Lord, give me the wisdom and patience to deal with distractions. Make me sensitive to the importance of the teaching moment. For Your sake and in Your name I pray. Amen.*

ENCOURAGE ONE ANOTHER DAILY,
AS LONG AS IT IS CALLED TODAY,
SO THAT NONE OF YOU MAY BE
HARDENED BY SIN'S DECEITFULNESS.
—Heb. 3:13

CORRECTION DOES MUCH, BUT
ENCOURAGEMENT DOES MORE.
—Johann Wolfgang von Goethe

ENCOURAGEMENT

Who are your encouragers, the people who pick you up when you're down on teaching? And whom do you encourage?

Every teacher needs a buddy list, a group of friends or fellow teachers who provide a shot in the arm now and then. Cultivate relationships with a few other leaders; it's like putting money in the bank. We're in a Great Commission army. Our Captain, Jesus, is leading us forward together. But He's not only our Captain—He's also our Elder Brother. We're part of a family, a community of brothers and sisters, who lift as well as love.

Your fellowship of encouragers also keeps you honest. If you're fortunate, not only will your friends and colaborers give you a word of praise, but they'll also give you an honest and helpful critique. There are times when a critique is more valuable than a compliment.

Pride has a way of blinding us to real needs. It's also a sin. And sin insidiously keeps us from being effective.

Prayer: *Lord, help me not only to be encouraged but also to be an encourager. Let me lift as well as love those who share the mission. In Christ's powerful name I pray. Amen.*

WHEN HE SAW THE CROWDS, HE HAD
COMPASSION ON THEM, BECAUSE THEY
WERE HARASSED AND HELPLESS, LIKE
SHEEP WITHOUT A SHEPHERD.
—Matt. 9:36

GOD'S CARE WILL CARRY YOU SO
YOU CAN CARRY OTHERS.
—Robert H. Schuller

SHEPHERDING

*P*eople need more than instruction: they need care. A teacher must be more than an "answer man" or "answer woman." A good teacher is also a friend, counselor, prayer partner, or mentor, as the situation demands.

What's the condition of your sheep? Are they tired and weary? Strengthen them. Are they rambunctious and wild? Rein them in. Are they hurting and lonely? Comfort them.

Many of your students will come from battlefronts. They've faced the terrors of the times. They've looked for support and found only criticism. In some cases they've looked for love and found only selfish lust.

They'll need someone to pour the healing oil of goodness into their lives and wounds, a shepherd who sees where they are, who understands their hearts, who'll go to where they are, who'll bind their wounds for Jesus' sake.

You are that person. You accepted the assignment to teach, but you were really given the task of shepherding.

Prayer: *Lord, give me eyes to see the needs of my class members. And give me Your compassion to bind their wounds and lift their fallen spirits. In Your name I pray. Amen.*

I AM THE GOOD SHEPHERD; I KNOW
MY SHEEP AND MY SHEEP KNOW ME.
—John 10:14

GOD HAS A PLAN FOR THIS BANKRUPT
WORLD. HE STILL HAS SOMETHING IN
STORE FOR IT. THIS DARK, SATANIC
EARTH, DROWNED IN BLOOD AND TEARS,
THIS EARTH OF OURS, HE STILL
WANTS AS A THEATRE FOR HIS
GRACE AND GLORIOUS DIRECTION.
—Helmut Thielicke

WHOSE SHEEP ARE THESE?

When I speak of "our" house, of course I don't mean it literally. For most of us, "our" house belongs to the bank, at least for a few more years! We're simply living there in increments of time, paying as we go. When the pastor speaks of "my church," he or she knows the statement isn't completely accurate. The Church belongs to Christ. He bought it with His own blood and supports it with His own power.

What we really mean is "the house I'm responsible for," and the pastor means "the church within my care."

So what does it mean when it's said the attendees on Sunday morning are "your" students? They belong to Christ; they're in your care. First, it means you're responsible for their religious education. Your knowledge of God's Word is communicated during relatively short intervals of time each week. Carefully study the Word. Carefully learn the teaching methods that will communicate the greatest amount of truth in the shortest span of time. Christ has given you the task of teaching His truth.

Second, it means you're an extension of His love. He will smile through your smile. He will embrace through your arms. He will welcome by your hand. His heart for the condition of your students will beat through yours. You're His onsite representative.

Always point "your" students beyond yourself; direct them to Christ. They aren't really yours. They're His, and you're His.

Prayer: *Lord, bring a renewed sense of responsibility to my heart. Help me see my class through Your eyes. And help me to nurture them by Your love. In Your wonderful name I pray. Amen.*

WE ARE HARD PRESSED ON EVERY SIDE,
BUT NOT CRUSHED; PERPLEXED,
BUT NOT IN DESPAIR; PERSECUTED,
BUT NOT ABANDONED; STRUCK DOWN,
BUT NOT DESTROYED.
—2 Cor. 4:8-9

DISAPPOINTMENTS THAT COME NOT
BY OUR OWN FAULT, THEY ARE THE
TRIALS OR CORRECTIONS OF HEAVEN;
AND IT IS OUR OWN FAULT IF THEY
PROVE NOT TO OUR ADVANTAGE.
—William Penn

DISAPPOINTMENT

*I*t's going to happen. Sooner or later you'll be disappointed. A promising student may fall away. A coworker may let you down. The church may not seem to value the work you're doing. You'll be heartsick. You'll want to quit.

You won't be the first or the last to be disappointed on the front lines of Kingdom work.

Old Testament prophet Elijah sat under a tree and prayed for God to take his life because of a ministry disappointment. New Testament giant Paul despaired that all his associates had abandoned him to go their own way. Part of being a faithful servant of the Lord is learning to cope with disappointments.

But disappointments have a good side. They're the very things that strengthen our bond with God. Even in the smallest setbacks, the Comforter, the Holy Spirit, is our constant companion. He whispers His encouragement. He fortifies us with divine promises. He cheers our victories and consoles our defeats.

Our disappointments also strengthen us. They cause us to stretch for new ways to teach old truths. They season us as leaders. They enhance our witness. They cause us to rely more on heaven and less on the world.

Decide the outcome. Determine that even the most perplexing disappointments will not result in a crushing defeat.

Prayer: *Lord, may Your patience and resolve flow through my spirit. Use the pressing times to mold me into a better worker in Your mighty kingdom. In Your name I pray. Amen.*

MY MESSAGE AND MY PREACHING WERE
NOT WITH WISE AND PERSUASIVE WORDS,
BUT WITH A DEMONSTRATION OF THE
SPIRIT'S POWER.
—1 Cor. 2:4

EARNESTNESS COMMANDS THE
RESPECT OF MANKIND. A WAVERING,
VACILLATING, DEAD-AND-ALIVE
CHRISTIAN DOES NOT GET THE RESPECT
OF THE CHURCH OR OF THE WORLD.
—John Hall

ELOQUENCE

Have you wondered whether you're a good enough speaker to hold your class's attention? You're probably not. Have you been nervous, thinking you don't know enough to be effective? You probably don't.

And here's the good news: you don't have to!

Wise and persuasive words aren't necessarily the same as effective communication. Some of the most eloquent politicians have lost elections by large margins. Teaching spiritual truth is not about eloquence—it's about anointing. If you're skeptical about this, read the biography of Uncle Bud Robinson.

Even when the searching or searing questions of your class leave you speechless, your very dependence upon God will give more answers than a hundred rehearsed phrases.

When Moses faced a sea of Israelites and confessed his lack of public speaking talents, God pressed Aaron into service to be His spokesperson.

God has what it takes to make your message effective. In fact, the message alone is eloquent. You're simply the line of communication He uses to communicate it!

You don't need to be eloquent—you just need to be dependent.

Prayer: *Lord, use my mouth, my hands, my eyes, and most of all my heart to be a channel of truth. In Jesus' name I pray. Amen.*

THERE IS A TIME FOR EVERYTHING,
AND A SEASON FOR EVERY ACTIVITY
UNDER HEAVEN.
—Eccles. 3:1

"NOW" IS THE WATCHWORD OF THE WISE.
—Charles Haddon Spurgeon

Timing

Why is it some class sessions seem to drag on and on while others fly by? Why are there some days when students seem eager to learn and other days when they seem to be bored?

There's a time for everything, and everything happens in its time. You can take advantage of that by learning to "read the seasons." The look of boredom, the restlessness, the distracting behavior—these are indications that it's time for Plan B. A wise teacher has more than one weapon in his or her arsenal. Some battlefront wars are won with cookies and Kool-Aid. Sometimes a cup of coffee has enough grace in it to soften the hardest heart.

You'll come to know when your students are ready to get serious and when they need some down time. You'll come to know when a detour is the best route available for reaching your teaching destination.

Going with the flow doesn't necessarily mean you've lost control. It simply means you're capitalizing on a learning "season." That's not a mandate for sloppiness or an excuse for lack of preparation. Rather, it's the realization that time and events can be used as powerful teaching tools.

Timing, as they say, is everything.

Prayer: *Lord, help me to be sensitive to the varying moods of my students. Give me wisdom to lead them without driving them. And help me to use the immediate to teach the eternal. In Jesus' name I pray. Amen.*

IF WE ARE THROWN INTO THE BLAZING
FURNACE, THE GOD WE SERVE IS ABLE
TO SAVE US FROM IT, AND HE WILL
RESCUE US FROM YOUR HAND, O KING.
—Dan. 3:17

A GEM IS NOT POLISHED WITHOUT
RUBBING, NOR A MAN MADE PERFECT
WITHOUT TRIALS.
—Chinese Proverb

IN THE FIERY FURNACE

ave you been there yet? Every teacher winds up in the fiery furnace sooner or later. A class discussion becomes heated. Emotions flare, and you're on the spot. A parent objects to your teaching activity. After church you face an angry confrontation.

There's a checklist for the teacher in the fiery furnace. First, remember that it's God's class, not yours. You're under His appointment. The Christian education council or the church board simply served as His commissioning agents. You're amenable to them—but ultimately you're amenable to *Him!*

Second, remember that you're doing the best you can. You're in the right place. You're doing the right things. You're teaching the right truth. Given the circumstances, few could face the situation with the grace you have shown.

Third, remember that you're teaching humans. Humans have as many quirks as they do qualities. They come from backgrounds as varied as snowflakes. They handle their hurts and hopes differently. And you're standing in the middle!

Are you in the fiery furnace? Don't sweat it. God's in control as always.

Prayer: *Lord, help me not to speak or act without first consulting You. In Jesus' name. Amen.*

I PLANTED THE SEED, APOLLOS
WATERED IT, BUT GOD MADE IT GROW.
—1 Cor. 3:6

IF YOU DON'T INVEST MUCH,
DEFEAT DOESN'T HURT AND
WINNING IS NOT EXCITING.
—Dick Vermeil

SOWER OR HARVESTER?

Everyone wants to be a harvester. Why not? Harvesting is fun! That's when you see the results: people respond, churches grow, souls are saved. What's not to like?

Sowing is hard work, and it takes faith. The sower spreads the seed *believing* it will be effective yet seldom *seeing* the results. The sower works in the changing seasons—with their accompanying challenges. The sower works day and night but seldom receives recognition.

You are a sower. God has placed the seed of His Word in your hands. He has called you to spread the seed over the hearts and minds of eternal souls, believing without seeing, working without recognition, and enduring the effects of the changing seasons.

And yet you sow faithfully week by week preparing lessons, calling on prospects, praying for students. Here's the important point: both the sower and the harvester are part of the same victorious team!

Heed the sign at the exit of some churches' parking lots: "You are now entering the mission field."

Prayer: *Lord, give me understanding to see that no part of Kingdom building is insignificant. Give me courage to keep sowing even when I know I won't be part of the harvest. In Your precious name I pray. Amen.*

HE REASONED IN THE SYNAGOGUE WITH
THE JEWS AND THE GOD-FEARING
GREEKS, AS WELL AS IN THE MARKETPLACE
DAY BY DAY WITH THOSE WHO
HAPPENED TO BE THERE.
—Acts 17:17

A MAN CAN'T ALWAYS BE DEFENDING
THE TRUTH; THERE MUST BE A
TIME TO FEED ON IT.
—C. S. Lewis

TOPICS

A good teacher can start from any subject. Paul was always ready to debate philosophy, religion, politics, or whatever was the buzz of the day. But his goal was always the same—to turn the conversation toward Jesus Christ.

What will spark the interest of your students? The teacher must be ready to jump in on any discussion. Family, sports, current events—you never know what will be on your class members' minds. Or you can bring a starter topic to present: the headline from today's newspaper, an anecdote from work, a question about dealing with in-laws. From these everyday topics you can launch into eternal matters.

Begin where your students are. No topic is off limits. Any road can lead your conversation to the gospel. And that's your ultimate destination. Sanctified sidetracks can be interesting, informative, and even inspirational, but you're first and foremost a teacher of the Good News. Christ's virgin birth, victorious life, vicarious death, and glorious resurrection must be the core topics. Current events are important only as they relate to the One who is "the same yesterday and today and forever" (Heb. 13:8).

Prayer: *Lord, open my eyes and ears to the interests of my students. And help me always to lead them to You. In Your name I pray. Amen.*

COME, SEE A MAN WHO TOLD ME
EVERYTHING I EVER DID.
COULD THIS BE THE CHRIST?
—John 4:29

YOU CAN HAVE IT ALL—EVERYTHING—
ON THE WIRE CALLED JESUS CHRIST.
THAT WIRE WILL NEVER SNAP. NOT
FOR A LIFETIME. NOT FOR ETERNITY.
—Charles R. Swindoll

A SINGULAR QUESTION

The Samaritan woman developed an instant passion for introducing people to Jesus. Already an outcast, she had no fear of offending the sensibilities of her neighbors. She was desperate to place this burning question before them: *Do you know Jesus?*

Indeed, that's the only question that matters in a person's life. That's the vital question for every man, woman, or child you'll ever teach. It's important that your students learn memory verses. It's good for them to learn theological concepts. But it's vital they know Christ personally.

Have you answered that question for yourself? Paul wrote about the personal spiritual discipline that influences others. "I beat my body and make it my slave so that after I have preached to others, I myself will not be disqualified for the prize" (1 Cor. 9:27). The "prize" was more important to him than his position. Whatever it took to lead a disciplined life—physically, emotionally, or spiritually—was well worth it if it resulted in living forever with Jesus. No service on earth can substitute for salvation.

Have you placed that question before your students? The faces in your classroom represent eternal souls—souls that will eternally perish or souls that will live forever in heaven.

No one ever flunked Sunday School. But someone in your class very well may hear the fateful words of the Savior: "I don't know you or where you come from. Away from me, all you evildoers!" (Luke 13:27). Better get acquainted now.

Prayer: *Lord, search my heart. I can't teach what I haven't first experienced. Then give me the wisdom and burden to introduce my class to Your eternal hope. In Your name I pray. Amen.*

ALWAYS BE PREPARED TO GIVE AN
ANSWER TO EVERYONE WHO ASKS
YOU TO GIVE THE REASON FOR
THE HOPE THAT YOU HAVE.
—1 Pet. 3:15

YOU NEVER GET TO THE END OF
CHRIST'S WORDS. THERE IS SOMETHING
IN THEM ALWAYS BEHIND.
THEY PASS INTO PROVERBS; THEY PASS
INTO LAWS; THEY PASS INTO DOCTRINES;
THEY PASS INTO CONSOLATIONS;
BUT THEY NEVER PASS AWAY.
—Arthur Penrhyn Stanley

THEOLOGY

*J*f God is good, then why do people suffer? Is Jesus really God? What is the penalty for sin? How do we know Jesus rose from the dead? These are theological questions, and people ask them every day.

Theology need not be frightening. Doing theology is nothing more than learning about God. As a teacher, you must be a theologian—one who has thought about who God is and what He's doing.

You don't need a master's degree to tackle theological issues. A simple childhood prayer at mealtime can be a treatise on one's understanding about God: "God is great. God is good." That's Theology 101. In times like these, the whole world needs to understand what you believe about God's greatness and goodness. Your knowledge of His attributes, for example, can be just what your students need to understand in order to trust Him in tough times.

And in a time of pluralistic philosophies, your class needs to know about that one way to heaven: Jesus Christ, who said, "I am the way."

When you read the Bible, pay attention to the big issues. Be familiar with the doctrinal writings of the Church. Talk theology with your peers, other Sunday School teachers. Have a question? Talk it over with your pastor.

Study the Word. Spend time in prayer. Read recommended books about the Christian faith. Your students need answers about your hope. They need your theology. Be prepared!

Prayer: *Lord, I want to know more about You. Give me a heart to study, and give me courage to share answers about the hope I've found in You. In Your powerful name I pray. Amen.*

You know that Timothy has proved
himself, because as a son with his
father he has served with me
in the work of the gospel.
—Phil. 2:22

People expect the clergy to have the
grace of a swan, the friendliness of
a sparrow, the strength of an eagle
and the night hours of an owl.
—Edward Jeffrey

HELPING MY PASTOR

*I*t's been said that being a single parent is the toughest job in the world. If that's true, then being a pastor is the second hardest. Pastors face the challenges of managing their churches all week and then must step into the pulpit on Sunday with a genuine word from the Lord. They enter into people's lives at funeral homes, wedding receptions, and graduation parties. They must challenge those who sin, offer grace to those who fall, and accept criticism from those who don't understand.

Your pastor needs your help.

As a Sunday School teacher, you can be a tremendous blessing to your pastor. You can reinforce his or her teaching to your students. Using a sermon illustration or main point from last week's message not only reinforces your lesson but also reinforces your students' thoughts about the ministry.

Praise your pastor's successes and defend his or her failures. You can't excuse those attitudes and actions that are contrary to God's Word. But you can help your students understand that pastors are people too. You are your pastor's "public relations director."

You can also help your pastor by offering a personal word of encouragement. He or she will benefit. So will you, and so will the gospel.

Prayer: *Lord, help me understand that I'm a member of a ministry team. And help me understand that my pastor is my coach. In Your name I pray. Amen.*

THEN AGRIPPA SAID TO PAUL, "DO YOU
THINK THAT IN SUCH A SHORT TIME YOU
CAN PERSUADE ME TO BE A CHRISTIAN?"
—Acts 26:28

A PERSON MAY GO TO HEAVEN WITHOUT
HEALTH, WITHOUT RICHES, WITHOUT
HONORS, WITHOUT LEARNING,
WITHOUT FRIENDS; BUT HE CAN
NEVER GO THERE WITHOUT CHRIST.
—John Dyer

SALVATION

$\mathcal{P}$aul was on trial for his life. That was not exactly the most opportune time to present the gospel. So what? Paul did it anyway. After all, how many times do you get to speak before a king?

In fact, the enemy of your faith will always try to convince you there's no appropriate time to share the plan of salvation. He's always trying to persuade the world there's a more convenient time—later. He is the lord of procrastination.

But the Bible says that the time for salvation is now. "'In the time of my favor I heard you, and in the day of salvation I helped you.' I tell you, now is the time of God's favor, now is the day of salvation" (2 Cor. 6:2).

In your Sunday School class, any time is an appropriate time to present the claims of Christ. Some in your class may not be believers, and this may be their most opportune time to hear the gospel. What a privilege it would be to lead a new soul into the Kingdom!

In fact, the Sunday School class could be one of the best places in the church to offer an invitation to salvation: the small group. Most likely, there will be other Christians present to lend support. You're talking about the Christian faith already. What could be more natural than to invite someone to accept Christ in that setting?

So go ahead—pop the question: "If you've not accepted Jesus Christ as your Savior, would you like to do it now? Why not pray along with me?"

Prayer: *Lord, impress upon my heart the importance of presenting the plan of salvation while there's still time for my class to hear about it. In Jesus' name I pray. Amen.*

FOLLOW MY EXAMPLE, AS I
FOLLOW THE EXAMPLE OF CHRIST.
—1 Cor. 11:1

A PERSON WHO LIVES RIGHT, AND IS
RIGHT, HAS MORE POWER IN HIS SILENCE
THAN ANOTHER HAS BY WORDS.
—Phillips Brooks

EXAMPLE

*W*as it conceit? Was it arrogance? Was it pride that caused the apostle to use himself as a "good example" for the Corinthian Christians?

No. It was just good teaching technique. People learn best by example. Paul gave them one.

The Christian life is built upon following examples. We call it *discipleship*. We emulate Jesus Christ. Others who are less mature imitate us. Mentoring is nothing more than good old-fashioned disciple-making.

How's your example? If your class members follow you, will they be on the right track? Is your faith prominently on display? Do you have the character qualities that are attractive to those who may be seeking? Will some child say, "When I grow up I want to be just like my Sunday School teacher"?

Who are you mentoring right now? Have you picked out a student or two and said, "Follow me"? You have not only the opportunity to teach a lesson but also the opportunity to influence lives. Your spiritual interest in your students may be just the thing to make them responsive to Christ's call. Your support of their spiritual gifts may be just the encouragement they need to exercise them.

Don't be afraid to think of yourself as an example to your students. You are one, whether you realize it or not. Do it intentionally, and do it well.

Prayer: *Lord, thank You for giving me the opportunity to shape a life as well as to teach a lesson. Help me do it with anointing and grace. In Your precious name I pray. Amen.*

IT IS GOD'S WILL THAT
YOU SHOULD BE SANCTIFIED.
—1 Thess. 4:3

AFTER SANCTIFICATION, IT IS
DIFFICULT TO STATE WHAT YOUR
AIM IN LIFE IS BECAUSE GOD HAS
TAKEN YOU UP INTO HIS PURPOSES.
—Oswald Chambers

SANCTIFICATION

When God saved you, He never intended to leave you as you were. He wanted you to be forgiven but also cleansed and changed. It's His will that you should be sanctified—set apart for His holy service and filled with His Pentecostal power.

Have you been sanctified? Have you surrendered your will fully to His? Have you allowed Him to create a pure heart in you? Far more important than presenting a lesson on sanctification is your experiencing it. It's not a vague or unreachable experience. It's simply presenting all that you know of yourself to all that you know of God. Giving your life as a living sacrifice (Rom. 12:1) will be the most important "next step" you'll ever take.

Have you called your students to that spiritual step? Have you presented the biblical truth that God desires their sanctification? Your knowledge of God's plan for completing His saints will help you in your age-level, maturity-level presentation. Ask the Holy Spirit to help you communicate the Spirit-filled life to your class.

Remember: sanctification is not a matter of being above temptation or human failings. It's a cleansing of the mind and heart that only God can do. And He wants to do it!

Prayer: *Lord, may I be Your instrument in telling my class how to go on to spiritual maturity. But first, search my heart for anything that would hinder the free flow of Your Spirit in my heart, my life, and my ministry. In Your name I pray. Amen.*

DO YOUR BEST TO PRESENT YOURSELF
TO GOD AS ONE APPROVED,
A WORKMAN WHO DOES NOT NEED
TO BE ASHAMED AND WHO CORRECTLY
HANDLES THE WORD OF TRUTH.
—2 Tim. 2:15

A MIST IN THE PULPIT DOES
CREATE A FOG IN THE PEW.
—Charles R. Swindoll

STUDY

*A*thletes can't get by without practice. If they're not in shape, it will show on game day. Actors can't make it without rehearsal. If they don't know their lines, performances will be punctuated by embarrassing mistakes and pauses. And teachers can't do without study. Few things are more uncomfortable than standing before a group of people—even a small Sunday School class—with inadequate preparation. You can't teach it if you don't know the material.

Do you have a regular time of study, a place and time that you use to prepare for your teaching experience? Busy as these days are, study habits must be created intentionally. Hectic schedules, ringing phones, "urgent" messages—don't let these interruptions lure you away from your regular study time.

God's redemption plan wasn't an improvisation. It was well planned, even before the beginning of time. "When the time had fully come, God sent his Son, born of a woman, born under law, to redeem those under law, that we might receive the full rights of sons" (Gal. 4:4-5). God is a God of order, of preparation. And He expects no less from His people.

Be faithful to your study time, and it will be faithful to you. You'll be confident, knowledgeable, and fully prepared to teach the Word.

Prayer: *Lord, I want to represent You prayerfully and carefully to my students. I commit myself to faithful preparation and diligent study. In Your matchless name I pray. Amen.*

I CONSIDER MY LIFE WORTH NOTHING
TO ME, IF ONLY I MAY FINISH THE
RACE AND COMPLETE THE TASK THE
LORD JESUS HAS GIVEN ME—
THE TASK OF TESTIFYING TO THE
GOSPEL OF GOD'S GRACE.
—Acts 20:24

AN ACRE OF PERFORMANCE IS WORTH
THE WHOLE WORLD OF PROMISE.
—James Howell

THE RACE

*I*n an automobile race the difference between finishing first and not finishing at all can come down to something very small: a few pounds of tire pressure, a bit of debris on the track, a gallon or two of gasoline. At 200 miles per hour, it doesn't take much to cause a bad day. Winning teams do sweat the small stuff. Everything has to be right.

We're in a race too. We're working feverishly to finish the course set out for us—making disciples of Jesus Christ. No need to worry about winning. Jesus already came in first! But we do want to finish the course. We want to present our lives and our work to Him in the winner's circle of heaven.

To do that, we'll have to determine to finish the course. At times the ministry of the gospel is similar to a 200-mile-per-hour race. There are more things to do than can be done, more places to go than can be gone to, and more people to see than can be seen.

And like a race, debris on the track can be dangerous—criticism, bad habits, lack of resources, and so on. But those who finish the course overcome the obstacles for the sake of the finish. They focus on winning and refuse the whining!

Are you on track to finish?

Do you diligently prepare for race day? Do you fuel your class sessions with prayer? Is your own spiritual life in "racing tune?" Like racing, teaching the gospel leaves little room for error. Run well. Finish the course.

Prayer: *Lord, thank You for the promise of a finished race. Thank You for the victory that's already mine. Now I ask You to give me courage and diligence to complete the course. In Christ's name I pray. Amen.*

YOU BECAME A MODEL TO ALL THE
BELIEVERS IN MACEDONIA AND ACHAIA.
THE LORD'S MESSAGE RANG OUT FROM
YOU NOT ONLY IN MACEDONIA AND
ACHAIA—YOUR FAITH IN GOD HAS
BECOME KNOWN EVERYWHERE.
—1 Thess. 1:7-8

GOOD IS NOT GOOD WHERE
BETTER IS EXPECTED.
—Sir Thomas Fuller

MAKING A DIFFERENCE

The reason you teach is obvious. You teach because of the teacher who made a difference in your life. Perhaps it was your primary class teacher, Mrs. Shook. She didn't babysit your class. She taught you about Jesus. You remember that she prayed with you. Or maybe it was your junior high class teacher, Mr. Johnson. He caught a lot of paper airplanes in the back, but he never minded. You knew he cared. It may have been Dr. McFarland, the teacher of your young adult class. No question was too tough for him. He taught you to think about what you believe.

From prekindergarten through senior adult, a troop of dedicated educators are faithfully teaching memory verses, leading discussions, and praying with students every Sunday morning. One or more of them made Jesus real to you. Now you're making Him real to someone else.

Some people live their entire lives wondering whether they've made a difference in the world. Sunday School teachers don't have that problem.

Prayer: *Lord, I want to thank You for the dedicated men and women who have shaped my life by their examples. Thank You for their prayers, their songs, their lessons, their interest. Give me, I pray, a heart like theirs. In Christ's name I pray. Amen.*

WHEN THE CHIEF SHEPHERD APPEARS,
YOU WILL RECEIVE THE CROWN OF GLORY
THAT WILL NEVER FADE AWAY.
—1 Pet. 5:4

HE WHO HAS NO VISION OF ETERNITY
WILL NEVER GET A TRUE HOLD OF TIME.
—Thomas Carlyle

THE CROWN

*Y*ou'll get your reward in heaven. That's not cheap senti-
ment. It's the simple truth for a Sunday School teacher.
You won't be paid for your work here, not unless setting up
chairs and picking up gum wrappers count as compensation.
And you'll get precious little thanks for your labor.

But there *is* a crown—your crown. It will be placed on
your head right after Jesus says the words "Well done, good
and faithful servant." It's the reward you get for being faithful
in your calling.

And there are stars in that crown. There's a star for John.
Yes, the same little Johnny who terrorized your junior class for
three years. He never heard a word. But he learned that God is
love, and he asked Jesus to come into his heart at the close of
one particularly trying class period. And there's a star for
Melody Grable's mother. No, you never met her. She never
came to your church. But she read the notes you sent home,
including the one titled "Sharing the Gospel with Your Child."
It was Melody's mom who got saved that day. She joined another congregation with her new husband. But she'll be in
heaven because of you.

Never doubt the value of what you're doing. So much of it
is unrecognized here. And you feel frustrated at times—another Sunday capping another week of preparation, another time
of straightening out the messes made by a thoughtless other,
another coping with the frustration of too much to do in too
little time. But you're not doing it for anyone here. You're doing it for Jesus. It will be worth it all.

And your crown will prove it.

Prayer: *Lord, give me a heart that understands the bottom line.
Keep my eyes focused on eternity instead of time. In Jesus' precious
name I pray. Amen.*

THE PEOPLE WERE AMAZED AT HIS
TEACHING, BECAUSE HE TAUGHT THEM
AS ONE WHO HAD AUTHORITY,
NOT AS THE TEACHERS OF THE LAW.
—Mark 1:22

THE SIMPLE SHEPHERDS HEARD THE
VOICE OF AN ANGEL AND FOUND THEIR
LAMB; THE WISE MEN SAW THE LIGHT OF
A STAR AND FOUND THEIR WISDOM.
—Fulton J. Sheen

THE MASTER TEACHER

They had never seen anything like it. Most teachers were master manipulators and able evaders. They reasoned and debated and discussed—but avoided stating a firm opinion.

Not Jesus. He taught with authority, like someone who knew what he or she was doing, someone who knew the truth.

And He made it plain. He used parables, stories from everyday life, to make big ideas understandable. He used questions and sayings and object lessons, anything to help people understand.

Does your teaching more resemble the teachers of the law, or Jesus? Do you teach with confidence? Are you able to make complex ideas understandable? Do you use a variety of teaching methods?

You can go to teaching seminars—and you should. You can study the latest methodology—and that will certainly be helpful. You can pop a video into the VCR and learn about teaching—and that will benefit your class.

But if you want to be a master teacher, you'll want to spend time with the Master. In your heart, you'll sit with Him in that little boat on Galilee as He teaches the crowds on the beach. You'll walk alongside Him as He points to a fig tree and teaches a brief lesson about fruitfulness. You'll inch closer to Him as He sits on the mountainside and teaches people how to walk victoriously through life.

Savior. Lord. Master. Son of God. These are perfectly descriptive names for Jesus. Here's one more: Teacher.

Prayer: *Lord, I want to be so much like You in my classroom ministry that others will plainly see the Master Teacher shining through me. In Your name I pray. Amen.*

THIS IS THE VICTORY THAT HAS
OVERCOME THE WORLD, EVEN OUR FAITH.
—1 John 5:4

IF ALL THINGS ARE POSSIBLE WITH GOD,
THEN ALL THINGS ARE POSSIBLE TO
HIM WHO BELIEVES IN HIM.
—Corrie ten Boom

Victory

The apostles might be surprised if they could listen to the testimony time in an average Sunday School class. These days we talk more about struggles than triumphs. We see ourselves as toiling laboriously at the impossible task of serving God and others. We focus on failure.

But the apostle John had a different idea. To him, Christians live a life of victory! We know Christ and have His power in us. We're children of the light. We live by faith. We're overcoming the world! Each toil has a potential triumph. Every pain has a potential comfort. Every despair has a potential hope.

Review your own victories. Has God enabled you to resist some temptation? Have you seen positive changes in your life? Is your faith stronger today than it was a year ago? Those times of reflecting on God's goodness and grace are strengthening times. You'll see up close that God hasn't failed you in the tough times.

Share those successes with your students. Along with teaching your class about the faith that works on the battlefronts of life, show them. Your witness to God's miracle-working power in your life will have a positive and lasting impression on their lives.

And give them opportunities to share their victories as well. There are times when students can teach the teacher. Their account of personal spiritual victories can be a great blessing to your own faith.

Prayer: *Lord, I praise You for the victories You've already helped me to win. You've been faithful in Your power and in Your presence. In Your name I pray. Amen.*

AQUILA AND PRISCILLA GREET YOU
WARMLY IN THE LORD, AND SO DOES THE
CHURCH THAT MEETS AT THEIR HOUSE.
—1 Cor. 16:19

FOR THE EARLY CHRISTIANS, KOINONIA
WAS NOT THE FRILLY "FELLOWSHIP" OF
CHURCH-SPONSORED, BIWEEKLY BOWLING
PARTIES. IT WAS NOT TEA, COOKIES,
AND SOPHISTICATED SMALL TALK IN THE
FELLOWSHIP HALL AFTER THE SERMON.
IT WAS AN ALMOST UNCONDITIONAL
SHARING OF THEIR LIVES WITH THE
OTHER MEMBERS OF CHRIST'S BODY.
—Ronald J. Sider

SMALL GROUPS

The early Christians didn't go to "super churches." Sure, they had large gatherings at Pentecost and a few other times. But most of the time they met in small groups—house churches.

Small groups have always been the place where Christians go for fellowship, prayer, and instruction. The large group has its function. But it's in small groups that dynamic life change happens.

No matter how large your Sunday School class may be, it's a small group. It's a microcosm within the larger church. It's a more personal setting for spiritual fellowship and accountability. Large or small, your class can be divided into several "houses." What may be too intimidating before a group of 15 or 50 may be just right with a group of 5 or 10.

Are you in a small group? Being part of a small group will accelerate your own spiritual growth—a group of fellow teachers, a Bible study group, a prayer circle. Interaction with Christians in an informal and intimate setting can be a great strengthening activity.

Are you creating small-group experiences for your students? Is your classroom a *forum* for your own ideas, or a *farm* where life applications are grown in the soil of truth among fellow growers?

Motivation, excitement, mass evangelism—these may happen in large groups. But life change happens in the small group.

Prayer: *Lord, teach me the value of being accountable to my brothers and sisters in the faith. And give me the opportunity to bring them together in a Spirit-led small group. In Your name I pray. Amen.*

ONE THING I DO: FORGETTING WHAT
IS BEHIND AND STRAINING TOWARD
WHAT IS AHEAD, I PRESS ON TOWARD
THE GOAL TO WIN THE PRIZE FOR
WHICH GOD HAS CALLED ME
HEAVENWARD IN CHRIST JESUS.
—Phil. 3:13-14

ONE OF THE HIGHEST AND NOBLEST
FUNCTIONS OF MAN'S MIND IS TO
LISTEN TO GOD'S WORD, AND SO TO
READ HIS MIND AND THINK HIS
THOUGHTS AFTER HIM.
—John R. W. Stott

FOCUS

$\mathcal{W}$hat's the most important thing in your life?

You might list your priorities as "God first, others second, myself last." "God first" would be a good focus.

Is that accurate? Look at these two infallible indicators of your prime concern: your planning book and your checkbook. Where are you spending your money and your time? That question will answer the first question—what's the most important thing in your life?

Paul's focus was simple. He wanted to serve Christ, and he had sacrificed every other thing in his life to that goal—career, money, relationships. Everything lined up after his top priority of following Jesus.

What are the things that bleed your time and money away from your goal to serve Christ? These other activities and interests are not evil in themselves. They become dangerous only when they began to wrestle your heart for control.

Do you need to sharpen your focus, reorder your priorities? Every day of the year can become "New Year's Eve." Spiritual resolutions filtered through the Word and the direction of the Holy Spirit can change your life.

Paul said, "One thing I do." What is your "one thing"?

Prayer: *Lord, more than anything else in my life, I want to focus on You. I want my teaching to reflect the importance of Your daily presence in my thinking and in my working. I pray in Your name. Amen.*

MAKE EVERY EFFORT TO LIVE IN PEACE
WITH ALL MEN AND TO BE HOLY;
WITHOUT HOLINESS NO ONE
WILL SEE THE LORD.
—Heb. 12:14

A HOLY LIFE WILL PRODUCE THE DEEPEST
IMPRESSION. LIGHTHOUSES BLOW NO
HORNS; THEY ONLY SHINE.
—Dwight Lyman Moody

HOLINESS

℮ very effect has a cause. That is seen in the advice from the writer to Hebrew Christians. The effects of the first, "peace with all men," come from the latter, "be holy." Without a pure cause there won't be a pure effect. It's the same in Christian ministry: a pure motive is paramount to pure effects. Ministry efforts may be very noble, but without a pure motive, or cause, they may have disastrous results.

Why are you doing the work of ministry? Is it from coercion? Obligation? Peer pressure? If that's the case, then every Christian work—including teaching a Sunday School class—will end in dreary monotony.

However, if your Christian service comes from a heart that seeks only to please Christ, then exciting and rewarding effects will be the norm. People-pleasers have no joy in their service. Christ-pleasers exude enthusiasm, even in the thickets of Christian service.

Check your heart even before you check your teacher's packet. Who's in charge? Christ? What or who is the force of your inspiration? The Holy Spirit? Holiness of heart is necessary not only for world peace but for any ministry. A heart free from selfishness and full of the Spirit of Christ is a heart aflame for ministry.

You may get along without being filled with the Holy Spirit. But the journey won't be much fun—especially if you're a preschool teacher and you run out of cookies!

Prayer: *Lord, most of all, I want a heart that's pure. My human efforts are nothing without Your holy zeal in them. In Jesus' name I pray. Amen.*

SINCE THROUGH GOD'S MERCY WE HAVE
THIS MINISTRY, WE DO NOT LOSE HEART.
—2 Cor. 4:1

GOD DID NOT CHOOSE US BECAUSE WE
WERE WORTHY, BUT BY CHOOSING US
HE MAKES US WORTHY.
—Thomas Watson

METHODS OR MINISTRY?

The flannelgraph has been packed away for years. In fact, even the blackboard is nearly a relic. New methods have replaced the old. Every year Christian publishers come up with a new slant on teaching timeless truths. But is Christian education just about methodology? Of course not. Christian education is about ministry—about raising men, women, boys, and girls into the image of the Lord Jesus Christ.

That's one of the easiest things to forget. You're not necessarily in the classroom because you're the best teacher or because you're knowledgeable about the best materials available. You're there because you have a burden for ministry. You've caught a glimpse of the soul's eternal destiny. You have everlasting truth for people caught in the web of time.

Ministry looks beyond the classroom. Its purpose is to communicate principles people will be able to use in factories, schools, offices, and family rooms to overcome evil and influence for good.

Methods are important, and sometimes the newer the better. People have moved beyond the flannelgraph to the brave new world of technology. But methodology must not be substituted for ministry. God has given us, first of all, a ministry. Because of what He did in our hearts, we try to bring about life change in our students.

Prayer: *Lord, I thank You for new technologies. But I thank You most of all for Your timeless truths. I'm glad You called me to ministry. In Your precious name I pray. Amen.*

DAY AFTER DAY, IN THE TEMPLE COURTS
AND FROM HOUSE TO HOUSE, THEY
NEVER STOPPED TEACHING AND
PROCLAIMING THE GOOD NEWS
THAT JESUS IS THE CHRIST.
—Acts 5:42

TEACH US THAT WEALTH IS NOT
ELEGANCE, THAT PROFUSION IS
NOT MAGNIFICENCE,
THAT SPLENDOR IS NOT BEAUTY.
—Benjamin Disraeli

SURROUNDINGS

You don't need a Crystal Cathedral to let the light shine through. Some of the greatest preachers and teachers of all time have been won to Christ in makeshift Sunday School classrooms, kitchens, furnace rooms, and pastor's studies. The facilities weren't ideal, but the impact was life-long.

What makes for ideal surroundings when it comes to Christian education? It takes more than brick and mortar, new carpet, fresh flowers, upgraded furniture, and a coffee urn.

Great surroundings start with a cheery smile. The first-century church made as much of an impact for Christ in their homes as they did in the Temple. Why? Because their hearts were on fire, and that fire made their faces glow! Over time, someone who really cares can warm the stoniest heart.

Neatness also speaks volumes. The tiniest kitchen classroom can be carefully arranged. The chairs can be lined up neatly. An attractively lettered welcome sign can be prominently placed. The Word of God is too important to be presented in a sloppy setting.

Great surroundings also include an atmosphere of spiritual concern. A spur-of-the-moment classroom can be a spiritual oasis. As long as the teacher has a burden to see class members won into the Kingdom, it really doesn't matter where the class meets. Some student's heart will be warmed by the invitation to accept Christ.

Prayer: *Lord, help me be more concerned about what happens in my class than where my class meets. In Your name I pray. Amen.*

WE PROCLAIM TO YOU WHAT WE HAVE
SEEN AND HEARD, SO THAT YOU ALSO MAY
HAVE FELLOWSHIP WITH US. AND OUR
FELLOWSHIP IS WITH THE FATHER AND
WITH HIS SON, JESUS CHRIST.
—1 John 1:3

BE TO THE WORLD A SIGN THAT WHILE
WE AS CHRISTIANS DO NOT HAVE ALL
THE ANSWERS, WE DO KNOW AND
CARE ABOUT THE QUESTIONS.
—Billy Graham

SHOW AND TELL

Teaching is more than sharing facts or theories—it's "show and tell." Just like the child bringing a treasure from home to share with the class, the teacher brings to the lesson his or her experiences. The apostles would have little sermon material had they not met Christ. But their walk with the Master gave them a briefcase full of beliefs based on their firsthand experiences.

Tired rhetoric about the "good old days" won't keep a class alert. Your class wants to know what God is doing in your life right now! Your fresh encounter with Jesus—something you have seen and heard recently—is the material for a great lesson.

Have you had a bad week salvaged by a promise from God's Word? Share it. Has your faith been stretched by a financial need? Tell how God supplied. Did the Holy Spirit bear witness to your heart, in spite of Satan's attacks, that you belonged to the Father? Let the class know. They don't need to hear all the gory details of your struggles with a skin rash, but they do need to see and hear about God's proactive mercy in your life.

The best "show and tell" is a heart brimming with love for Jesus. Your class will stand in awe of that, far more than of your recitation of memorized Bible verses. Your testimony of a fresh meeting with the Heavenly Father in prayer and meditation on His Word will create more spiritual want-to than a promised picnic at the end of the quarter.

As Jesus said, "Let your light so shine before men, that they may see your good works, and glorify your Father which is in heaven" (Matt. 5:16, KJV).

Prayer: *Lord, let my meetings with You be the light that illuminates my classroom. In Your wonderful name I pray. Amen.*

WHEN YOUR CHILDREN ASK YOU,
"WHAT DO THESE STONES MEAN?"
TELL THEM THAT THE FLOW OF THE
JORDAN WAS CUT OFF BEFORE THE
ARK OF THE COVENANT OF THE LORD.
. . . THESE STONES ARE TO BE A MEMORIAL
TO THE PEOPLE OF ISRAEL FOREVER.
—Josh. 4:6-7

I AM A PART OF ALL THAT I HAVE MET.
—Alfred, Lord Tennyson

GENERATION TO GENERATION

*E*ach Olympic event is preceded by a very moving tradition. Torches, lit by the flame of a common source, are carried from city to city to the place of the Olympic event. Celebrities and commoners alike thrill to be the one who will carry the torch for a prescribed number of feet or miles. It's a great media event. The runner with the symbolic torch arrives at a certain location where another runner is waiting. The runner extends the torch's flame to light the torch of another.

Joshua was instructed to make such a transfer. He didn't use a flame, however. He used stones. His job was to tell the next generation about God's salvation from the situations of Israel's journey.

Did you ever think of Christian education as landscaping? Each week, in orderly fashion, you lay out stones for your class: stones of truth passed along from another, stones of mercy seen in the lives of those before you, stones of salvation or sanctification taught by godly men and women who have influenced your life.

You're landscaping a path of hope for the next generation. From generation to generation, the gospel message is kept alive because someone like you dared to put down a stone, a monument to the greatness and the grace of God.

Prayer: *Lord, keep me conscious of what I'm doing in my class each week—passing the torch of truth along. In Christ's name I pray. Amen.*

NOW THERE WERE STAYING IN
JERUSALEM GOD-FEARING JEWS FROM
EVERY NATION UNDER HEAVEN.
—Acts 2:5

I AM NOT BORN FOR ONE CORNER; THE
WHOLE WORLD IS MY NATIVE LAND.
—Seneca

CROSS CULTURE

First Church is teaching a class on English as a second language. Trinity Church has a Hispanic congregation meeting in its facilities. Calvary Church has a Bible study for Asians.

What are they doing? Missions.

You don't have to go very far to be a missionary these days. God-fearing people (and those who don't fear Him) from all over the world are bringing the mission field to your local community. Gone is the time when mission outposts were found only in remote jungles. Now it can be in your very class. You can open your heart and your facilities to people searching for Christian fellowship, instruction, and service.

Vocational missionaries are still vital to fulfilling the Great Commission. But a whole new cadre of missionaries is being formed. They work 9 to 5 in secular employment, but they have another job as well. They are part-time missionaries in the local church, reaching out to a vast new population, arrived from various ports of call to your location.

New citizens by the scores are looking for a helping hand with a new language, new customs, new housing, new vocations. They need someone to show them around. And often they carry more than a suitcase. They carry the baggage of loneliness, guilt, or sin.

There you are: a servant of Christ in the right place—the Sunday School classroom—at the right time.

Prayer: *Lord, make me sensitive to the mission field in my own hometown. And help me to do my part by introducing people to Christ as well as introducing them to local customs. In Your powerful name I pray. Amen.*

AS HE APPROACHED JERUSALEM AND
SAW THE CITY, HE WEPT OVER IT.
—Luke 19:41

AFFLICTIONS MAKE THE HEART MORE
DEEP, MORE EXPERIMENTAL,
MORE KNOWING AND PROFOUND,
AND SO, MORE ABLE TO HOLD,
TO CONTAIN, AND BEAT MORE.
—John Bunyan

TEARS

hat's more important? Toil or tears? By His very life, Jesus said both. His approach to Jerusalem was in His job description. He was coming to town to teach the world how to love the unlovely and forgive the unforgiving. In a matter of hours, He would offer His life for every man's sin. But His task brought sudden tears.

Probably every teacher has been on the brink of tears: by the frustrations of inadequate class space, unruly students, too little time to adequately prepare, lack of support.

But there's also a different tear: that of a heart broken by the lost condition of a student. It's a Jesus kind of weeping, shedding tears for the sin of a city, for individuals content to go along with the crowd.

Those tears are fitting for the toil of the Sunday School leader. The students filling the chairs in your classroom aren't numbers—they're souls. They will be eternally lost without a personal faith in Christ. Pray for them. Maybe this week's lesson will be their last opportunity to accept the gospel message. Maybe these are their final moments for learning about God.

Sure, you'll need to be faithful in your preparation. But you'll also need to be faithful in your praying. Teaching like Jesus will mean weeping like Jesus, shedding tears of sorrow over the sin of those you love.

Prayer: *Lord, put a tear in my eye for the soul's condition of my students. In Your name I pray. Amen.*

SELLING THEIR POSSESSIONS AND GOODS,
THEY GAVE TO ANYONE AS HE HAD NEED.
—Acts 2:45

A CHRISTIAN SHOULD ALWAYS REMEMBER
THAT THE VALUE OF HIS GOOD WORKS
IS NOT BASED ON THEIR NUMBER AND
EXCELLENCE, BUT ON THE LOVE OF GOD
WHICH PROMPTS HIM TO
DO THESE THINGS.
—Saint John of the Cross

RELIEF EFFORTS

The outpouring of gifts and goods for the survivors of the September 11, 2001, attack on the United States was overwhelming. Finally, the relief agencies had to issue a request: "Don't send any more food or clothing." It's not a modern phenomenon. The Early Church had the same kind of heart—and even greater. It didn't take a disaster for them to open their food pantries to the hungry. They didn't collect clothing simply because there was a national calamity. Efforts of relief were simply an extension of their faith.

Come to think of it, your Sunday School class can be a relief agency. Week in and week out, you could be the source of someone else's support in the church or in the community. A lesson on compassion has no better illustration than a collection of canned goods for a family whose house has been destroyed by fire. The message of forgiveness can't be taught with more power than when a class decides to adopt the family of a prisoner and give Christmas gifts.

What can you do? Jesus already made out a checklist (Matt. 25). Visit the institutionalized. Share clothing. Look after the sick. Make provisions for the homeless. Distribute food and water.

That relief effort could be just the thing to revitalize your class. And if you take the leadership, it will certainly revitalize you.

Prayer: *Lord, show me those in my community who have needs my class and I can meet for Your sake. In Jesus' name I pray. Amen.*

"THOUGH THE MOUNTAINS BE SHAKEN
AND THE HILLS BE REMOVED, YET MY
UNFAILING LOVE FOR YOU WILL NOT BE
SHAKEN NOR MY COVENANT OF PEACE
BE REMOVED," SAYS THE LORD,
WHO HAS COMPASSION ON YOU.
—Isa. 54:10

CHRISTIAN LOVE LINKS LOVE OF GOD
AND LOVE OF NEIGHBOR IN A TWOFOLD
GREAT COMMANDMENT FROM WHICH
NEITHER ELEMENT CAN BE DROPPED.
—Georgia Harkness

Loving Influence

Week after week, they walk softly into your classroom. They almost drop into the folding chairs. They're visibly worn and wounded, bruised and battered by trauma and loss. God has an unfailing love for them. And so do you. Without you and God, they're loveless and friendless. You're their link to the Father. You're His loving influence in their lives, His source of peace in their world of war.

What an opportunity! With your caring, tender words, deeds of kindness, and sympathy, they'll have new hope. Fifty-two times each year they'll have an opportunity to come to the place where you teach to hear about the Savior's love. And even more times than that, you'll have the opportunity to go where they are—by phone, by E-mail, or in person, to show them the Savior's love.

As a teacher you have great influence, not simply because you have a file folder full of facts about Bible times or Bible characters. Rather, you're influential because you're an ambassador of the kingdom of Christ. You represent His concern as well as His cause. You gather little children to yourself as He did. You go to the suffering or sorrowing as He did. You represent heaven at an earthly wedding as He did. You offer a shoulder to the weeping as He did.

Teachers are the loving influence.

Prayer: *Lord, give me arms wide enough to reach around the hurts of my class. In Your name I pray. Amen.*

NOT THAT I HAVE ALREADY OBTAINED ALL
THIS, OR HAVE ALREADY BEEN MADE
PERFECT, BUT I PRESS ON TO TAKE HOLD
OF THAT FOR WHICH CHRIST JESUS
TOOK HOLD OF ME.
—Phil. 3:12

EVERYONE SHOULD HAVE A GOAL FOR
WHICH HE IS WILLING TO EXCHANGE
A PIECE OF HIS LIFE.
—Carlyle Boehme

BREAKING THROUGH THE WALL

$\mathcal{L}$ong-distance runners know about it. There's an invisible wall that must be broken through if the race is to be successful. Those who give it one more effort, who dig deep for another last-gasp lunge toward the finish line, are said to have "broken through the wall."

All runners can start the race. All runners can buy the running shoes and fill out the questionnaire. All runners can wear their numbers and stand in the appointed rows, waiting for the starter's pistol to sound. But not every runner who starts a race will finish it.

Some will quit because they're too weak. They don't have the right nourishment. They don't eat right. They neglect to hydrate themselves. They simply don't have enough strength to go another mile.

Some will quit because they're discouraged. Other runners are too far ahead of them. They don't see any use trying to reach a finish line that so many others in front of them have already crossed.

But some, just like you, will determine to "break through the wall." They'll refuse to give up. They'll continue to make every effort to reach their destinations. Why? Because they're following the Lord Jesus Christ. They press on because He did. They reach out because He reached out to them.

Your race is unlike any earthly one. You're racing against time. You have only a few weeks or years to lead your class to a level of spiritual maturity that will see them through tough times.

You're racing to win souls, to disciple believers, and to commission workers for the Kingdom.

Never quit. Never.

Prayer: *Lord, I give You my life, my love, and my service to do what You called me to do in this precious moment of time. In Your name I pray. Amen.*

ABOUT THE AUTHORS

Stan Toler is senior pastor of Trinity Church of the Nazarene in Oklahoma City and hosts the television program *Mission Today.* For the past several years he has taught seminars for the INJOY Group—a leadership development institute. Toler has written over 45 books, including his best-sellers *God Has Never Failed Me, but He's Sure Scared Me to Death a Few Times; The Five-Star Church;* and his latest book, *The Buzzards Are Circling, but God's Not Finished with Me Yet.* His Beacon Hill books include *The Harder I Laugh, the Deeper I Hurt* and the Lifestream Resource series.

To Contact Stan Toler
Stan Toler
P.O. Box 892170
Oklahoma City, OK 73189-2170
E-mail: stoler1107@aol.com
Website: www.stantoler.com

John Baldwin is State Senior Credit Officer of AmSouth Bank in Tampa, Florida. He serves as Sunday School superintendent and chairman of the Evangelism/Discipleship Committee for the board of Highland Park Church of the Nazarene in Lakeland, Florida. For more than 10 years Baldwin has led adult Sunday School classes and Bible study groups. He has contributed devotionals to *Come Ye Apart* and authored numerous Bible study materials.

To Contact John Baldwin
John C. Baldwin
P.O. Box 3370
Tampa, FL 33601-3370
E-mail: merfb@aol.com